50
COMMON MAMMALS
OF THE SOUTHWEST

George Olin

WESTERN NATIONAL PARKS ASSOCIATION
TUCSON, ARIZONA

WARNING: *You should never touch or even closely approach any of the animals listed in this book. If you do, the animal may defend itself and bite or otherwise injure you. The publisher and authors accept no liability for any injuries or damages you may receive while acting upon or using the contents of this publication.*

Library of Congress Cataloging-in-Publication Data
Olin, George.
    50 commom mammals of the Southwest / George Olin.
        p. cm.
    Incudes bibliographical references (p.).
    ISBN 1-58369-006-9 (alk. paper)
    1. Mammals--Southwest, New. I. Title: Fifty common mammals of the Southwest. II. Title.

QL157.S69 O45 2000
599'.0979--dc21

00-044665

The net proceeds from WNPA publications support educational and research programs in your national parks.

Receive a free Western National Parks Association catalog, featuring hundreds of publications. Write or email:
www.wnpa.org
Western National Parks Association
12880 N. Vistoso Village Drive
Tucson, AZ 85737

Written by: George Olin
Updated, expanded, and revised by: Sarah Gustafson
Editorial: Abby Mogollón
Design: Campana Design
Illustration: Barbara Terkanian
Printed in China
Cover photograph: Paul Berquist

*A*t first glance, the Southwest might seem a bleak and barren place. Compared with greener country, this land of little rainfall and extreme summer heat hardly seems a mecca for mammals.

But appearances can be deceiving. Within historic times, the Southwest has harbored some two hundred species of native mammals—an abundance rivaled by few regions of comparable size. A brief sojourn here reaps many rewards, not the least of which are an awareness of the area's austere beauty, an appreciation for its diversity, and an understanding of the way native animals adapt to arid environments.

Stephen J. Krasemann/DRK Photo

WHAT IS THE SOUTHWEST?

The geographic scope of this book extends from western Texas to the coastal range of California, and from central Utah and Colorado to northern Mexico. It ranges in elevation from California's Death Valley, situated below sea level, to peaks of the southern Rockies that exceed fourteen thousand feet. Given such topographic extremes, local climates vary dramatically, as do the plants and animals that inhabit various parts of the region.

Southwestern habitats include forests, woodlands, grasslands, and riparian areas, but the region is best known for its deserts. Within this general area are portions of five distinct deserts: Chihuahuan, Sonoran, Colorado, Mojave, and Great Basin. Though each is characterized by different plant communities, all share what has been called a "grand

fact of dryness." Precipitation is scant and unpredictable. When rains do arrive, they are typically either so gentle that much of the moisture evaporates or so torrential that most of the water runs in sheets across the soil's surface rather than saturating the ground.

Because desert air contains so little water vapor, the sun penetrates it easily, sending ground surface temperatures soaring. With little moisture to hold in heat, the air cools quickly after the sun goes down. In the lower deserts, day and nighttime temperatures sometimes vary by fifty degrees Fahrenheit or more.

Although other habitats in the Southwest receive more precipitation than its deserts, they are generally arid relative to similar habitats in other parts of the continent.

To survive in the Southwest, some mammals have evolved physical and behavioral traits that help them stay cool and hydrated. Many avoid the heat of day by resting in shade or retreating to underground burrows. The Southwest awakens at night, when a variety of animals come out to find food.

Without water, *Homo sapiens* will die of thirst after only four days. Many southwestern species can survive much longer than that without drinking by obtaining most of the water they need from the plants and animals they eat. Some rely primarily on water created as a byproduct of digesting carbohydrates, and others conserve moisture by reabsorbing water from urine and feces.

Desert forms of widely distributed species may meet their water needs by staying closer to riparian areas than their counterparts in moister climes. Desert dwellers are often lighter in color than their kin, as well. In addition to blending in with sandy soils, pale fur reflects light and thus helps prevent overheating. Another physical feature shared by some of the area's mammals is oversized ears, which provide large areas of bare skin that dissipate heat.

OBSERVING MAMMALS IN THE SOUTHWEST

Visitors to the Southwest may at first be surprised to see so few animals during the day. As mentioned previously, most mammals save their activities for the cool hours between dusk and dawn. A quiet, nocturnal vigil with a flashlight can prove rewarding. Do not expect to see many mammals on windy nights; the noise of the wind and rustling branches hides the sound of predators, causing most prey to remain under cover. The greatest animal activity follows the first summer rains.

Most wild mammals avoid humans. However, you can frequently see their signs, such as diggings, scat, or tracks left in soft sand, mud, or snow.

If you're fortunate enough to catch more than a quick glimpse of a wild animal, enjoy it from a distance, as most are easily disturbed by human attempts at interaction. For their safety as well as your own, do not try to feed them. In addition to being nutritionally unhealthy, exposure to human foods can radically alter wildlife behavior. Above all, respect animals' privacy, and their ability to fend for themselves, and minimize your impact on *their* habitat.

Marty Cordano

For excellent opportunities to see mammals, as well as many plants, reptiles, and birds, visit the following natural areas:

ARIZONA

Canyon de Chelly National Monument
Casa Grande Ruins National Monument
Chiricahua National Monument
Coronado National Memorial
Grand Canyon National Park
Montezuma Castle National Monument
Navajo National Monument
Organ Pipe Cactus National Monument
Saguaro National Park
Tonto National Monument
Walnut Canyon National Monument
Wupatki/Sunset Crater Volcano National Monument

COLORADO

Black Canyon of the Gunnison National Park
Curecanti National Recreation Area
Great Sand Dunes National Park and Preserve
Mesa Verde National Park

NEVADA

Lake Mead National Recreation Area

NEW MEXICO

Bandelier National Monument
Capulin Volcano National Monument
Carlsbad Caverns National Park
Chaco Culture National Historical Park
El Malpais National Monument
Gila Cliff Dwellings National Monument
White Sands National Monument

OKLAHOMA

Chickasaw National Recreation Area

TEXAS

Big Bend National Park
Big Thicket National Preserve
Guadalupe Mountains National Park
Lake Meredith National Recreation Area

In addition, the Southwest is home to many national wildlife refuges, national forests, state and county parks, and private preserves, which are all good places to find mammals. Many visitor centers compile species lists that tell you which animals live in that preserve.

This book is designed to help the amateur naturalist learn about and identify southwestern mammals. Although the title says *common*, we've sneaked in a few that are scarce or currently absent but are interesting ecologically or even because of their rarity. These include once-important predators such as the gray wolf and black-footed ferret, as well as the armadillo and opossum, two unusual mammals that may be expanding their ranges into this region.

To identify a species using this book, pay close attention not only to its photograph and physical description, but to the range and habitat information as well. Some of the animals included occur only in specific areas or habitats of the Southwest. Others have a much broader range that encompasses this region.

We also mention particular habits that make identification easier, so don't forget to observe what an animal is doing as well as what it looks like. And keep in mind that size and coloration vary between individuals; the measurements and shades listed herein are not definitive.

Common and scientific nomenclature follows the *Revised Checklist of North American Mammals North of Mexico, 1997* by Jones and others. With apologies to mammalogists, we've taken liberties with the order of entries. We've included only one or two major species within each genus, synthesizing material from a variety of sources. For more information on these or other southwestern mammals, consult the readings listed at the back of the book.

We hope this guidebook will enhance your experience of the Southwest and encourage efforts to preserve and manage the area for its wild inhabitants. Predator control programs, overhunting, overgrazing, habitat destruction, and other encroachments of civilization have decimated local populations of many wildlife species. As extinctions increase, the importance of native wildlife and its conservation becomes both more apparent and more urgent.

1 · Bighorn Sheep
Ovis canadensis

These native sheep are named for the males' massive coiled horns, which serve as status symbols during the breeding season. Composed of a bony core covered by keratin, the horns continue to grow throughout the sheep's life, eventually weighing as much as thirty pounds. The females' horns are much shorter, slimmer, and only slightly curved. Both sexes have brownish-gray hair (not wool) and a conspicuous white rump patch.

For most of the year, rams roam separately from ewes and their young. Bachelor groups disband in late summer, when males join female flocks and begin battling for dominance. Rival rams display their horns, then rear on their hind legs, drop, and collide head-on with a bone-jarring crash that can be heard a mile away. To the larger, stronger victors go most of the mates.

ENDANGERED

Paul Berquist

One of the bighorn's keys to survival is its ability to escape in rugged, sometimes vertical terrain. Its cloven hooves consist of hard, horny shells with rough, resilient centers that provide excellent traction.

In arid regions, bighorn require access to drinking water, along with suitable escape terrain near foraging sites. Hunting, disease, and habitat intrusion have greatly diminished local bighorn populations; in many places, only scattered bands remain. Many states are conducting transplant operations to reestablish bighorn herds in former ranges.

SIZE	Total length about 63 inches, tail about 4 inches; weight, 100 to 300 pounds
HABITAT	Rocky ridges and cliffs in mountainous and canyon-cut country
RANGE	Formerly in foothills and mountains throughout the Southwest; isolated populations now found in eastern New Mexico, southern Colorado, and western Texas, along with mountainous areas of the West from northern Mexico to central British Columbia
ALSO KNOWN AS	mountain sheep

2 · Pronghorn
Antilocapra americana

SIZE	Total length about 53 inches, tail about 5 inches; weight, 90 to 130 pounds
HABITAT	Grasslands and sagebrush plains
RANGE	Throughout the Southwest and much of the western United States, extending into northern Mexico and southern Canada
ALSO KNOWN AS	antelope, pronghorn antelope

Although its generic name means "antelope goat," the pronghorn is neither. Whereas goats belong to the same family as bison and sheep, and antelope are found only in the Old World, this North American native is the sole surviving member of an ice-age group that included about a dozen species.

Males and most females bear distinctive horns, consisting of a bony core covered by a black outer sheath. Unlike other horned mammals, the pronghorn sheds this sheath annually. The does' horns, if present, are but a few inches long. Those of the buck average a foot in length and feature the forked ends that give this mammal its common name. The body is buff-colored, with two white bands across the throat, white underparts, and a prominent white rump patch that can be erected as a visual signal to others.

The fastest mammal in North America, the pronghorn can sprint at more than fifty miles per hour and cruise for several miles at more than half that speed. They roam open, rolling country in large herds, relying on powerful eyesight and speed for protection. In winter, a herd may drift more than a hundred miles in search of food. Because pronghorn rarely leap over barriers, fences can restrict their annual migrations, leading to starvation in severe weather.

Once numbering in the millions, America's pronghorn population plunged to some thirteen thousand animals in the early 1900s. Wise management has helped it recover in parts of its former range.

Paul Berquist

Paul Berquist

3 · White-tailed Deer
Odocoileus virginianus

C. Allan Morgan

This widely distributed deer was an important source of food and clothing for Native Americans and pioneers throughout much of the continent south of Hudson Bay.

Small and graceful, the whitetail takes its name from its long, broad tail, which is brown above and white below. In flight, it holds its tail high, displaying the white flag that signals danger and may alert fawns to the mother's location. In contrast to the mule deer's evenly branched antlers, whitetail racks consist of a main beam that curves sharply forward, with individual tines rising from it.

Although considered a browser, the whitetail varies its diet of leaves and twigs with grasses, herbs, and acorns. It forages furtively, ever alert. When startled, it hoists its tail and bolts. It does not bound as the mule deer does, but can run up to forty miles an hour and is a strong swimmer.

Does give birth to one, two, or occasionally three fawns in late spring. Though newborns can stand on wobbly legs within an hour or so, they remain hidden in vegetation for the first few weeks. Their spotted coats blend well with the dappled light of the forest floor, and their lack of noticeable odor make them difficult for predators to detect. With the mother returning to nurse several times a day, the fawns grow rapidly, tripling their birth weight within a month.

SIZE	Total length about 67 inches, tail about 10 inches; weight, 50 to 200 pounds
HABITAT	In the Southwest, mainly in wooded or brushy country, riparian areas, and broken terrain
RANGE	Southeastern Arizona, southwestern and eastern New Mexico, western Texas, eastern Colorado; extending throughout much of the United States
ALSO KNOWN AS	whitetail

4 · Mule Deer
Odocoileus hemionus

SIZE	Total length about about 63 inches, tail about 7 inches; weight, 100 to 350 pounds, adult males average 150 pounds
HABITAT	In the Southwest, from desert shrublands to coniferous forests; prefer broken country and/or vegetation that provides cover, such as brush or forest edges
RANGE	Throughout the western United States, northern Mexico, and southwestern Canada
ALSO KNOWN AS	black-tailed deer, burro deer

Named for their huge ears, mule deer are dark gray in winter and reddish brown in summer. A large, white rump patch surrounds a small, black-tipped tail that gives rise to another common name: black-tailed deer. As with other members of the deer family, the male grows and sheds antlers annually. In this species, the antlers branch in pairs, each fork of which may divide further into twinned points.

Where the mule deer's southwestern range overlaps with that of the white-tailed deer, the former occupy open, arid areas, while the latter prefer mountain forests. The two are easily distinguished by their hind ends and antlers. Furthermore, the mule deer runs with a distinctive, stiff-legged gait in which all four feet leave the ground and land in unison. When startled, it may travel some distance, then stop to look over its shoulder. In contrast to *O. virginianus,* which usually runs for cover, *O. hemionus* seeks open, broken country, where it can bound with ease over rocks and brush that impede pursuers.

Most active in the early morning and late evening, these deer are browsers, preferring leaves and twigs to grass. Without predators to keep their numbers in check, mule deer populations tend to fluctuate wildly. In times of plenty, populations increase until the deer eat themselves out of house and home. Major die-offs follow, and vegetation may take years to recover.

Paul Berquist

5 · Elk
Cervus elaphus

SIZE	Total length about 90 inches, tail about 6 inches; weight, 400 to more than 1,000 pounds, usually about 600 pounds; antlers up to 5 feet long
HABITAT	Mountain meadows and open, forested areas in summer; foothills and valleys in winter
RANGE	Higher mountains of western United States and southern Canada
ALSO KNOWN AS	*wapiti* (Shawnee), red deer (in Europe)

Males of many species expend a great deal of energy showing off for females, and the bull elk is no exception. Every summer, it produces a set of antlers used to attract and fight over mates. When the breeding season is over, these bony structures fall to the ground, where the abundant minerals they contain may be recycled by rodents. Contrary to popular belief, the size and number of points on an elk's rack is much more a function of physical condition than of age.

For most of the year, cows and young calves live in matriarchal herds of ten to several hundred, migrating from lowlands in the winter to mountain meadows in the summer. Come fall, the bulls join the herds, and begin bugling and sparring to attract as many cows as possible. For the next six weeks or so, a successful male spends most of his time either breeding the members of his harem or keeping other bulls from doing the same. After the rut is over, the exhausted bulls go off by themselves to recuperate.

The largest local member of the deer family, the elk is reddish brown, with a pale yellow rump patch surrounding its small, white tail. The dark hair on its neck forms a long, shaggy mane, and the large, branching antlers sweep backward over the shoulders.

The story of elk populations in the Southwest is one of decline, reintroduction, and—in places—exponential recovery to unnaturally high levels.

6 · Collared Peccary
Pecari tajacu

John Cancalosi

From a distance, this hoofed mammal resembles the domestic hogs and wild boars from which its family diverged at least forty million years ago. But unlike true pigs, peccaries are native to the Western Hemisphere, where their shallow rooting habits do not unnaturally disturb the environment.

Black and gray bristles blend to form a "salt-and-pepper" color across the peccary's back and sides. A lighter band of hair around the heavy-set neck forms the "collar" of its common name. The peccary is commonly known in the Southwest by the Spanish name, *javelina*, in reference to the males' tusks, which are short, straight, and razor-sharp.

With its tough, disk-shaped snout, the peccary turns over dead vegetation in search of roots and shoots. Its favorite foods include mesquite beans and the fruits and pads of prickly pear cactus. The latter—eaten spines and all—allow the peccary to go for days without drinking water.

These extremely social animals live in herds of five to fifteen or more. A diverse vocabulary of grunts, snorts, and clicks, combined with musk produced by a large rump gland, help individuals communicate within and between groups. Within a day or two of birth, a young peccary is able to follow its mother as she joins the herd to forage.

Peccaries have poor eyesight but a keen sense of smell. At the first scent of danger, they freeze, emit musk, and click their tusks. Though they may charge if cornered, they are more apt to flee in all directions. Tales of peccary "attacks" are more likely the animals' confused efforts to escape danger.

SIZE	Total length about 36 inches, tail about 1.5 inches and unnoticeable from a distance
HABITAT	In the Southwest, desert grasslands and brushy foothills, usually near water
RANGE	Southern Arizona and New Mexico, western and southern Texas; south to Argentina
ALSO KNOWN AS	*javelina* (Spanish), musk hog

7 · Jaguar
Panthera onca

ENDANGERED

C. Allan Morgan

The largest cat in the Americas, the jaguar ranks behind only the Old World tiger and African lion in size. This massive feline is muscular, with a heavy neck, broad face, and long tail. Dark rosettes spot its short, golden coat. Normally reserved around humans, the jaguar has an unearned reputation for ferocity.

From accounts of the early Spanish explorers, it appears jaguars were once common in parts of the Southwest. But large carnivores require substantial hunting ranges. As the region was settled, the cat's territory came into conflict with that of cattle ranchers. Some jaguars learned to prey on livestock, with disastrous results for the species. By the early 1900s, the United States had lost all of its breeding populations. Biologists believe the rare sightings from recent times to be of individuals that have wandered north from Mexico.

Like the mountain lion, the jaguar does not depend on speed to capture its prey. It will crouch on a limb overhanging a game trail and wait until a deer or other large mammal passes. With a spring, it drops on the animal's back, taking it to the ground under its great weight. An excellent swimmer, it also dines on fish, turtles, and other aquatic organisms. In the Southwest, the jaguar's former range coincided with that of the collared peccary, one of its favorite prey species.

SIZE	Total length up to 8 feet, tail up to 30 inches; weight, 100 to 300 pounds
HABITAT	Prefers to be near water. In the Southwest, jaguars once occupied desert grasslands and lower mountains
RANGE	Formerly in the Southwest and southeastern Texas, along both coasts of Mexico, and southward to Argentina; now rarely seen in the United States
ALSO KNOWN AS	*el tigre* (Spanish)

⁸· Bobcat
Lynx rufus

SIZE	Total length about 33 inches, tail about 5 inches; weight 15 to 35 pounds
HABITAT	Rocky and broken terrain with sufficient stalking cover, such as scrublands and open forests
RANGE	From southern Mexico, throughout most of the United States, into southern Canada
ALSO KNOWN AS	wildcat, bay lynx, barred bobcat, pallid bobcat, red lynx

Named for its stubby tail, the bobcat is larger than its domestic cousins but smaller than other wild cats in the region. It has large paws, tufted ears, and a reddish-tan coat scattered with dark spots and stripes. It often holds its short tail up, displaying the white tip underneath. Though seldom seen, the bobcat is fairly common in many parts of the Southwest.

If approached by people, a bobcat will lie perfectly still, depending on its protective coloration to escape detection. If routed from its resting place, it will run for cover with a somewhat stiff-legged gait. Although capable of great speed for short distances, it soon tires.

Lacking endurance, this nocturnal hunter relies on stealth rather than pursuit, crouching in wait beside a game trail to make a capture. Its keen eyes, ears, teeth, and claws make it a formidable predator. While it feeds mainly on rabbits and small rodents, it will occasionally kill young deer and pronghorn, along with insects and ground-nesting birds.

By the time bobcat kittens are six weeks old, they spend many waking hours pouncing on and wrestling with siblings in their den deep among rocks or brush or in a hollow log. When their mother brings home a small animal, more serious encounters ensue as each kitten attempts to capture the entire prize. At about two months, the kittens further sharpen their hunting skills by joining their mother on short nocturnal forays.

9 · Mountain Lion
Puma concolor

Stephen J. Krasemann/DRK Photo

The mountain lion's range once exceeded that of any other American mammal, extending from southeastern Alaska to southern South America and spanning the continental United States. Overhunting and habitat destruction have confined this secretive and solitary cat to large tracts of remote terrain.

The male's territory averages a hundred square miles and may overlap with the smaller home ranges of several females. Mountain lions mark their territories with "scrapes"—visible mounds of dirt, needles, and twigs that are often scented with urine or feces.

Though the habits of mountain lions vary from high mountains to desert to tropical jungle, their appearance is similar. As indicated by the name *concolor,* the cat's tawny coat is a monotone shade across most of its body, with lighter areas under the belly and inside the legs. It holds its tail—which is long, cylindrical, and may be tipped in black—close to the ground.

This highly efficient predator dines mainly on deer, helping to keep herds within the limits of their food resources. It stalks its prey, pouncing with full weight from close range. After making the kill, the lion drags the carcass to a secluded spot to gorge. When satiated, it covers the remaining meat with leaves and soil, bedding near the carcass by day and returning nightly to feed.

SIZE	Total length about 78 inches, tail about 30 inches; weight, 100 to 200 pounds
HABITAT	Almost any habitat with sufficient topographic or vegetative stalking cover. In the Southwest, it favors edges of rimrock country, where scrub desert ends and forest begins
RANGE	Throughout the western United States, Mexico, and southeastern Canada
ALSO KNOWN AS	cougar, catamount (short for "cat of the mountains"), puma, panther

10 · Common Hog-nosed Skunk
Conepatus mesoleucus

SIZE	Total length about 26 inches, tail about 9 inches
HABITAT	Brushy or sparsely timbered portions of desert foothills, washes, and canyons
RANGE	Southeastern Arizona, southern New Mexico, southeastern Colorado, southern Texas; south throughout most of Mexico
ALSO KNOWN AS	hognose skunk, rooter skunk, white-backed skunk, badger skunk, conepate

As its common name implies, this skunk has a pig-like nose pad on the end of its long, hairless snout. Its coarse coat is white above and black below, and its bushy, white tail contains scattered black hairs. Both lack the luster of those of other skunks.

The hog-nosed skunk roots through leaf mold and soft loam in search of food. With its specialized snout and large claws, it unearths insects, grubs, and worms, leaving characteristic patches of "plowed" soil and overturned rocks. Although classified as a carnivore, it's too slow to catch many vertebrates. Instead, it gleans the remainders of other predators' kills or eats whatever small rodents or reptiles it comes across.

Rustling noisily through dry leaves, this skunk ploddingly pursues its nocturnal activities with apparent indifference to its surroundings. When threatened, it typically runs for the cover of a bush or cactus. If pursued, it will hiss, stomp its front feet, raise its tail, and—if absolutely necessary—spray.

A skunk of desert valleys and brushy canyons, this species' range is shrinking due to the encroachment of civilization on its habitat. When displaced from its rooting grounds, it may not be able to adapt to alternative, unfamiliar habitat.

Marty Cordano

11 · Striped Skunk
Mephitis mephitis

Marty Cordano

"Noxious odor" is the English translation of *mephitis,* used not once, but twice in naming this most widespread and abundant of North American skunks. By contracting the muscles around its anal scent glands, the striped skunk can spray its musk several times in rapid succession, hitting a target more than twelve feet away.

Armed with such memorable defenses, striped skunks have few natural enemies. Although skunks are inoffensive if left alone, most potential predators associate the animal's coloration with its repulsive discharge. Great-horned owls and other raptors—which reportedly have little sense of smell—pose one chief threat. Automobiles present another. Road kills are a common sight (and smell) along southwestern highways, perhaps because these slow-footed animals are attracted to roads in their search for carrion and other foods and are not accustomed to being attacked.

The striped skunk is about the size of a house cat with a large, bushy tail. Its body is black, with a narrow white stripe down the center of the forehead and a white hood that divides into two white dorsal stripes at the neck, forming a V.

This nocturnal omnivore dens among rocks, under buildings, or in burrows dug in soft soil or abandoned by other mammals. Though often solitary, it may den communally during the winter.

SIZE	Total length about 28 inches, tail about 11.5 inches
HABITAT	Woodlands, brushy areas, and grasslands
RANGE	Throughout much of the United States, northern Mexico, and southern Canada
ALSO KNOWN AS	skunk, polecat

12 · Hooded Skunk
Mephitis macroura

SIZE	Total length about 26 inches, tail about 14 inches
HABITAT	Rocky or brushy areas in lower canyons and valleys
RANGE	Southeastern Arizona, southwestern New Mexico, and west Texas; extending southward throughout most of Mexico
ALSO KNOWN AS	white-sided skunk, southern skunk, *zorrillo* (in Mexico)

This skunk's "hood" consists of a ruff of long, usually white hairs on its neck and head. It has a thin white stripe between its eyes, and one to three white stripes running along its black back, sides, and tail. The color ratio of its upperparts is extremely variable, ranging from almost all black to almost all white. The hooded skunk's tail accounts for more than half its total length, giving rise to the specific name *macroura*, which means "long-tailed."

An expert hunter, this desert skunk pursues prey throughout the night. In its search for beetles and other insects, it scratches beds of leaf mold, digs around the base of shrubs and cholla, and turns over flat rocks. It also investigates clumps of grass that might shelter a bird's nest, along with nooks and crannies likely to conceal a rodent. At dawn, it retires to a burrow or deep crevice among the rocks to sleep the day away.

Young skunks accompany their mother on her nocturnal forays, often parading behind her in single file. The entire group frequently engages in mock battle, with the skirmishes occasionally escalating to a baring of teeth and claws, accompanied by monkey-like chittering cries.

Marty Cordano

13 · Western Spotted Skunk
Spilogale gracilis

SIZE	Total length about 16 inches, tail about 6 inches
HABITAT	Rocky and brushy areas from cactus desert to pines
RANGE	Throughout most of the western United States, extending into Mexico and southwestern British Columbia
ALSO KNOWN AS	civet cat, hydrophobia cat, phoby cat, polecat

Like all skunks, S. gracilis is equipped with a pair of anal scent glands that can discharge a foul-smelling spray to temporarily disable a pursuer. Basically peaceful, the skunk relies on its striking black-and-white coloration and behavioral displays to warn off predators, using its chemical weaponry only as a last resort.

This kitten-sized skunk has silky fur and a bushy, white-tipped tail. Its body is jet black, with four to six white stripes along its back and sides that break into spots on the rump. Spilogale, which means "spotted helmet," may refer to the white triangle in the middle of its black forehead. The origin of the common name "hydrophobia cat" is more difficult to determine, as this agile animal does not avoid water.

Anyone who travels Southwest deserts will likely meet this nocturnal nomad eventually. The social success of this introduction will depend almost entirely on the human element. Do not attempt to pick up Spilogale by its tail, as stories that claim it is defenseless in this position are false. Don't approach too closely if the skunk seems nervous, and slowly retreat if it begins to stamp its front paws in alarm. As a final warning, the spotted skunk may do a "handstand" on its front feet, prominently displaying its back and tail. At this stage, any startling movement or sound may cause it to resort to defensive measures distressing to all concerned.

C. Allan Morgan

14· Northern River Otter
Lontra canadensis

Allan and Sandy Carey

This semi-aquatic member of the weasel family has a long, cylindrical body covered with dense, waterproof fur. The muscular, tapered tail serves as oar or rudder in the water and aids in balance on land. The otter propels itself underwater either by undulating its lithe body or by paddling its powerful, webbed feet. Its nostrils and small ears close underwater, and its pulse slows during a dive, allowing it to remain submerged for several minutes.

The male otter usually lives alone, defending a large territory from other males, especially during the spring breeding season. The female gives birth to two to five pups, typically in a bankside den lined with dry vegetation and accessed via an underwater entrance. The young remain with her for about eight months. During the course of a year, this wanderer may range many miles along its waterway. If necessary, it will travel overland to reach another lake or stream.

The river otter dines primarily on fish, frogs, crayfish, and other aquatic invertebrates, as well as birds and their eggs. It hunts primarily by night, searching for prey under rocks and logs and in mud, or swimming along the water's surface seeking movement below.

Renowned for its playful nature, the river otter cavorts down snow-covered or muddy banks, runs and slides on snow and ice, plays "catch" with pebbles, and has been known to tease beavers with a bite to the tail.

SIZE	Total length about 43 inches, tail about 16 inches
HABITAT	Permanent bodies of freshwater and coastal wetlands; in the Southwest, found only along lakes, rivers, and perennial streams
RANGE	Historically found in riparian areas throughout North America, now limited to west-central Arizona, the Colorado River drainage, northwestern New Mexico, and southern Colorado
ALSO KNOWN AS	river otter, otter

15 · American Badger
Taxidea taxus

Built for life underground, the badger is broad and heavy, with a flattened appearance and a wedge-shaped head. Its legs are short and its front feet armed with stout claws up to two inches long. Distinct dark "badges" offset white cheeks and a white stripe that extends from the nose, between the ears, to at least the shoulder area.

This powerful digger is often mistaken for a large rodent because of its burrowing habits. Nevertheless, it is a member of the weasel family and possesses the irritability and predatory traits of that group. Though more inclined to retreat than fight, it growls and hisses menacingly if cornered, advancing at once upon any threatening movement. Its long, raking claws and sharp teeth make it a formidable opponent, and most predators avoid it.

The badger feeds primarily on large rodents and is especially valuable for controlling gophers and ground squirrels. If its keen nose tells it that prey is nearby, the badger will dig out the burrow to capture the occupant. Whether unearthed in pursuit of a rodent or used as a den, these holes are typically wider than they are high and oval in shape, evidence that the badger has excavated them.

These solitary animals are seldom seen together except during the breeding season. Several cases, however, have been recorded of badgers and coyotes traveling together.

Erwin and Peggy Bauer

SIZE	Total length about 31 inches, tail about 5 inches
HABITAT	Treeless terrain from low deserts to alpine meadows; prefers deep alluvial soil
RANGE	Throughout the Southwest; extending across the western two-thirds of the United States and far into Canada and Mexico
ALSO KNOWN AS	North American badger, *tlalcoyote* (in Mexico)

16 · Black-footed Ferret
Mustela nigripes

SIZE	Total length about 20 inches, tail about 5 inches
HABITAT	Prairie-dog towns
RANGE	Formerly throughout the plains of North America from northern Mexico to southern Canada; extirpated from the Southwest and perhaps limited to reintroduced populations in the upper Midwest
ALSO KNOWN AS	ferret

One of North America's rarest mammals, the black-footed ferret once ranged throughout the grasslands and basins of the central United States. This species illustrates well the dependence of one animal upon another. An inhabitant of prairie-dog towns, the ferret feeds primarily on that rodent and uses its burrows for shelter and nursery dens.

The extermination of prairie dogs and destruction of their habitat for agriculture and rangeland have left few towns large enough to support the ferret, now a federally endangered species and possibly extinct in the wild. Biologists began a captive breeding program in 1986 in the hope of replenishing and returning this predator to its natural habitat.

Due to the ferret's rarity and nocturnal, ground-dwelling nature, little is known of its life history. About the size of a mink, it is buff-colored, with black feet, a black-tipped tail, and a black mask. It likely takes its name—which comes from an Old French word for thief—from the latter.

Like other weasels, the ferret is long, cylindrical, and lithe. Able to climb trees and enter any burrow into which its head fits, it can pursue its prey almost anywhere. Its preference for prairie dogs notwithstanding, it also captures other small rodents and birds. When hunting kangaroo rats, it will glide down one entrance and reappear quickly at another, giving the impression that there are several ferrets in one burrow.

ENDANGERED

17 · White-nosed Coati
Nasua narica

SIZE	Total length about 41 inches, tail about 20 inches
HABITAT	Oak woodlands and adjacent grasslands
RANGE	Southeastern Arizona, extreme southwestern New Mexico and Texas; into Mexico
ALSO KNOWN AS	coatimundi, hog-nosed coon, *gato solo* and *solitario* (Spanish terms for adult males)

"Wistful" is a word some use to describe the coati's face, which is long and narrow, with a dark mask and small, brown eyes. Its slender body is rusty brown; its long, flexible snout terminates in a piglike pad of gristle; and its lengthy tail has inconspicuous dark and light rings. With its weight distributed between the toes and soles of its feet, it walks with a shuffling gait resembling that of a bear.

Holding its nose down and its tail straight up, the coati roots through beds of leaves and soft loam to unearth small mammals and reptiles, insects, worms, and tubers. With long, curved front claws, it overturns large rocks, digs in soil, and shreds dead logs to expose its prey. A talented climber, it takes to the trees when alarmed or to forage for fruits, berries, and bird eggs. Like a squirrel, it uses its tail for balance when leaping from limb to limb, and it can descend either head or tail first.

Unlike its closest relatives—raccoons and ringtails—coatis are diurnal and gregarious. They live and forage in bands of four to fifty, typically composed of adult females and their young. At about two years of age, males leave the bands and live alone, rejoining a group just for the breeding season.

C. Allan Morgan

18 · Mexican Raccoon
Procyon lotor

Marty Cordano

This intelligent mammal was named in two languages for its manual dexterity: "raccoon" comes from an Algonquin word for "he who scratches with his hands," and *lotor* means "the washer" in Latin. The latter refers to the animal's habit of manipulating its food underwater before eating it. Biologists now believe the raccoon may wet its fingers to enhance its sense of touch, not to cleanse its catch. Other identifying characteristics include a black mask, ringed tail, and hunchbacked stance.

The raccoon prefers to forage in or near water, leaving tracks resembling a child's handprint in the soft mud along streams. It might be seen crouching by the edge of a pool, looking vacantly into space while its fingers busily explore the streambank for a frog. A small pile of shells on a rock may mark the spot where a raccoon has been opening and eating crayfish and other aquatic invertebrates. An omnivore, it also consumes a variety of seasonally available plant material, using its front feet to pick fruits and nuts or to strip husks from ears of corn.

The raccoon sleeps by day and rears its young in a hollow tree or the crevice of a rocky bluff. The cubs commonly share the den until they are fully mature, even though this makes for crowded quarters.

SIZE	Total length about 35 inches, tail about 12 inches
HABITAT	Rough canyons and wooded areas near running water
RANGE	Throughout much of the United States and Mexico, into southern Canada
ALSO KNOWN AS	'coon

19 · Ringtail
Bassariscus astutus

SIZE	Total length about 30 inches, tail about 15 inches
HABITAT	Cliffs, rocky canyons, and other broken terrain; also found along brushy arroyos in the lower desert
RANGE	Throughout the Southwest
ALSO KNOWN AS	miner's cat, band-tailed cat, civet cat, coon cat, ring-tailed cat, bassarisk, *cacomistle* (Nahuatl)

A cousin of raccoons and coatis, the ringtail resembles many species but can be directly compared to none. Several common names ending in "cat" reflect the slender body; small, round feet that leave catlike tracks; finesse at climbing; and ambush-and-pounce hunting strategy. Ringtails earned the moniker "miner's cat," for instance, from early prospectors who kept them in their cabins to control mice.

But for its prominent eyes and rounded ears, the ringtail's face looks like that of a fox, and its scientific name means "clever little fox." Most conspicuous is its raccoon-like tail. As long as the head and body combined, the bushy tail is a beautiful combination of about seven black and seven white rings terminating in a black tip.

Though common in favorable habitats and active year-round, the ringtail is strictly nocturnal and thus rarely seen. Its sharp claws and ability to turn its hind feet backwards for traction enable it to scale trees, walls, and steep ledges. By dark of night, it prowls the crevices of rocky cliffs in search of rodents and insects. It spends little time off the ground, taking to the trees only to bag roosting birds or their eggs.

Marty Cordano

20 · Black Bear
Ursus americanus

Tim Fitzharris

A regular visitor to many mountain campgrounds, the black bear normally does not live up to its ferocious reputation. Though it will defend itself, its cubs, or its food supply, it usually retreats from people unless lured by food. According to the National Center for Health Statistics, you and I are 350 times more likely to be killed by lightning than by *U. americanus*.

Despite its name, this bear comes in many colors, from pure white to totally black. In the West, most are brown, cinnamon, or tan. All are heavily built, with small eyes and short, round ears. As with members of the raccoon family, the bear places its entire foot on the ground, leaving tracks roughly the size and shape of a human footprint, only wider and with claw marks. Strong and surprisingly agile, the black bear climbs trees, swims, and can sprint more than twenty-five miles per hour.

Black bears feed on a wide variety of fruits, nuts, and vegetation, along with insects, meat, and garbage. To store fat for winter dormancy, it must eat almost continuously throughout the summer and fall. Though black bears mate in June or July, implantation is delayed until late in the year, when the female is already asleep in her den. Two or three tiny, altricial cubs are born just a couple of months later. They remain with their mother until the fall of their second year.

SIZE	Total length about 63 inches, tail about 3.5 inches; weight, 220 to 330 pounds, occasionally up to 500 pounds in old males
HABITAT	Forests and woodlands
RANGE	Relatively remote, wooded areas throughout North America north of central Mexico; displaced by civilization from much of its former range
ALSO KNOWN AS	cinnamon bear

21 · Common Gray Fox
Urocyon cinereoargenteus

Paul Berquist

This mammal's graceful bearing, big ears, and large, bushy tail clearly identify it as a fox. Though sometimes confused with the red fox due to its cinnamon-colored sides and neck, the gray fox can be recognized by its silvery gray back and the black ridge and tip on its tail. It speaks with a loud bark, similar to that of a small dog, and its eyes glow a brilliant yellow-green if caught in a flashlight's beam.

Secretive and nocturnal, the gray fox rests in a secluded place by day and hunts widely through the night. Although it prefers a diet of rodents, this omnivorous animal consumes a wide variety of insects, small vertebrates, and whatever fruits and vegetables are seasonally available. Its indiscriminate appetite allows the gray fox to live where predators with more specific needs could not.

This canid employs some hunting techniques more characteristic of cats. Lacking a coyote's speed, the fox is more likely to sneak up on its prey, striking with both paws to pin its victim to the ground. It is a master of the ambush and will crouch motionless for hours along a rabbit trail. An adept climber, it may scale a fifty-foot tree to seek refuge, to rest, or to forage on fruit. Although it usually dens in a rocky cleft or underground burrow, the gray fox has been known to raise its young in hollow trees, sometimes far above ground.

SIZE	Total length about 38 inches, tail about 14 inches; weight, 7 to 15 pounds
HABITAT	Open forests, brushy woodlands, and rocky canyons
RANGE	Throughout the United States and Mexico, excluding portions of the Great Plains and mountainous West
ALSO KNOWN AS	tree fox, *zorra gris*, *gato de monte* (Spanish)

22 · Kit Fox
Vulpes macrotis

SIZE	Total length about 30 inches, tail about 12 inches; weight, 3 to 6.5 pounds
HABITAT	Deserts and desert grasslands
RANGE	Throughout much of the Southwest, excluding north central Arizona, northeastern New Mexico, and much of southern Colorado and Utah
ALSO KNOWN AS	desert fox

Macrotis, which means "large eared," aptly describes this yellow-gray fox. Not much bigger than a large house cat, the kit fox is North America's smallest wild canine. Its oversized tail, tipped in black, accounts for up to 40 percent of its total length. This denizen of the desert Southwest is closely related to the swift fox *(V. velox),* found east of the Rio Grande and across the Great Plains.

Their catlike agility and swiftness make these small foxes adept at catching whatever rodent or hare is most common in the vicinity. In some areas, they prey almost entirely on kangaroo rats. And like some kangaroo rats, the kit fox has fur-covered toes that give it traction in soft sand and loose soils.

Unlike most male mammals, canid fathers take an active part in raising their young. Though not as social as their larger cousins, kit fox pairs stay together throughout the breeding season and may mate for life. They build a cluster of dens, typically in alluvial soils under mounds of earth designed to prevent flooding. The dens have many entrances and are connected by spiraling tunnels that provide habitat for potential prey.

Kit foxes emerge from their dens shortly after sunset to hunt and are rarely seen during the day. Curious and relatively unsuspicious, they are easy targets of traps and poisons intended for other predators.

C. Allan Morgan

23 · Gray Wolf
Canis lupus

SIZE	Total length about 66 inches, tail about 18 inches; weight, 50 to 175 pounds
HABITAT	Browse and grassland areas where ungulates live
RANGE	Once found throughout most of North America; now limited to Canada, Alaska, northernmost portions of the United States, and the Sierra Madre of Mexico. In the Southwest, reintroduced in Arizona and New Mexico
ALSO KNOWN AS	timber wolf, prairie wolf, *lobo* (Spanish)

The largest of the canid family, the gray wolf resembles a big German shepherd. Heavy through the neck and shoulders, and taller in front than in back, it appears to crouch. Compared with its cousins, the wolf has long legs, a short tail, and a broad head.

These highly social animals live and hunt in tightly knit packs of family members dominated by a mated pair. The mother stays with her six or so pups for about two months, while the father and other pack members bring home food. Adapted to run for hours on end, wolves travel great distances in pursuit of deer, elk, and other large prey.

To communicate within and between packs, wolves employ a variety of howls and other vocalizations, postures, facial expressions, and tail movements. They also scent-mark their large territories with urine and feces, creating olfactory fences easily detected by other wolves.

Perhaps no other mammal has undergone such an ambivalent relationship with humankind. Long ago, people tamed and selectively bred wolves, developing today's domestic dogs. But in recent centuries, the wolf's taste for ungulates has put it at odds with human interests. When buffalo—once this predator's primary food source in the West—were exterminated, wolves turned to cattle and other livestock. Vigorous predator-control campaigns launched in the early 1900s have eliminated wolves from the southern portion of their former range. As a result, unnaturally high populations of deer and elk now take a heavy toll on vegetation.

ENDANGERED

Lynn Rogers

24 · Coyote
Canis latrans

SIZE	Total length about 47 inches, tail about 14 inches; weight, 15 to 45 pounds
HABITAT	Almost every life zone and any type of terrain
RANGE	Once found primarily in the West and Great Plains, the coyote now occurs throughout most of North America. It is common in the Southwest
ALSO KNOWN AS	prairie wolf, brush wolf, song dog, melon wolf

Larger than a fox and smaller than a wolf, the coyote looks much like a medium-sized dog, but its muzzle is more pointed and its black-tipped tail is bushier. When running, it holds its tail between its legs. The coyote is most active around dawn and dusk but may be seen throughout the day. Because members of the canid family are aggressive toward their smaller cousins, wolves, coyotes, and foxes rarely coexist in any given area.

Adaptable and opportunistic, the coyote survives in almost any habitat, from mountain meadows to the streets of Los Angeles. Despite being the target of intensive predator-control programs, this trickster of many Native American legends continues to thrive. It has expanded its range over the last century into portions of the continent once ruled by the now-extirpated wolf.

The coyote earned its scientific name, which means "barking dog," for the diverse repertoire of barks, yaps, growls, and howls it uses to communicate with fellow coyotes. Loosely structured packs usually consist of a breeding pair and their young, but the coyote's social behavior changes with seasons and size of prey. The male helps raise the pups, supplementing their milk diet first with regurgitated solid food, later with whole animals.

Fast enough to catch jackrabbits, coyotes typically hunt alone when small prey are available. They will team up if needed to catch deer or other large game. In addition to fresh meat, these omnivores eat everything from carrion and garbage to fruits and roots.

Paul and Shirley Berquist

25 · Common Porcupine
Erethizon dorsatum

Paul Berquist

The porcupine's distinctive armor inspired its name, which is Latin for "quill pig." This large rodent has thousands of loosely attached, spiny hairs covering its back, sides, and tail. White with black tips and mixed with dark underfur and yellowish guard hairs, they give the animal a shaggy, salt-and-pepper appearance. The feet have long, curved claws that aid in climbing trees.

Contrary to popular belief, the porcupine does not "throw" its quills. When cornered, it lowers its head, erects its quills, and keeps its back toward the enemy. At the slightest touch, it flails its tail from side to side, driving dozens of quills into the pursuer's flesh. Held in place by their barbed points, the quills work in deeper and may eventually kill the recipient. Mountain lions, coyotes, and bears are among the few predators that successfully attack porcupines, flipping them to expose their unprotected bellies.

The porcupine's gait is a slow, deliberate waddle interrupted by pauses to sniff and perhaps nibble a plant. It divides its time between trees and ground, with a semi-permanent den typically located among large rocks. One young is born in the spring. Its quills harden within a few hours of birth.

It may be surprising that the porcupine—associated with coniferous forests of the north—occurs commonly in piñon-juniper woodlands and uncommonly in the lower desert of the Southwest. At lower altitudes devoid of conifers, it eats mesquite beans and grass, browses on low shrubs, and may strip some bark from mesquite and ironwood trees.

SIZE	Total length about 35 inches, tail about 8 inches
HABITAT	Most common in montane forests, but can survive almost anywhere there are trees
RANGE	Widely distributed throughout the western United States and much of Canada
ALSO KNOWN AS	quillpig, hedgehog, *puerco espin* (Spanish)

26 · White-throated Woodrat
Neotoma albigula

SIZE	Total length about 13 inches, tail about 6 inches
HABITAT	Wide range of arid habitats, from brushlands to rocky ledges to low desert; prefers areas with stands of cacti
RANGE	Throughout most of the Southwest
ALSO KNOWN AS	trade rat, packrat

The white-throated woodrat is best known for its weather-tight den, consisting of an above ground nest covered by a spiny fortress of sticks, cactus parts, and found treasures. Scientists study ancient dens—some thousands of years old—for clues to an area's prehistoric vegetation and climate.

The nest is a marvel of construction, with thick, warm walls woven of shredded bark or coarse grass, lined with softer fibers. Upon dismantling a typical protective mound, biologists inventoried numerous paloverde sticks, cow chips, tin cans, joints of various cacti, pieces of newspaper, and a fruit jar lid. In excess of $7\,1/2$ ounces, the largest stick weighed more than the average woodrat.

This species often builds its nest among cholla or prickly pear cacti, which offer protection as well as food and water. An excellent climber, it scales the cacti, removing sharp spines to scatter around its home to deter predators. As the woodrat dines primarily on cactus and woody vegetation, it can nibble on its den during food shortages.

Both the body and tail of this rodent are brown above and white below. As its name implies, its throat is pure white. Its ears are large and naked, and its tail is thick and round.

Attracted to shiny objects, woodrats often drop what they're carrying to pick up a more-appealing item. Because they appear to barter sticks for people's trinkets, some call them "trade rats."

Marty Cordano

27 · Grasshopper Mouse
Onychomys spp.

SIZE	Average total length, 5 to 6 inches, tail 1.5 to 2 inches
HABITAT	Desert grasslands and scrub with sandy or gravelly soil
RANGE	Throughout the Southwest, also across the Midwest and much of the Great Basin
ALSO KNOWN AS	calling mouse, scorpion mouse

Like a meat-lover in a family of near-vegetarians, the grasshopper mouse fills a different niche than that of its relatives. While most mice are carnivorous to a small degree, this vicious predator dines mainly on grasshoppers, scorpions, and other arthropods. Sometimes hunting in small groups, it also eats fellow rodents up to three times its size, killing them with a bite to the neck.

Grasshopper mice share many behavioral traits with true carnivores. They have complex courtship rituals and live in close family groups. The male takes an active role in caring for the pups. Relatively nomadic, they may usurp the burrows of other small mammals. They mark their large territories with scent, defending them aggressively against intruders. To communicate with each other over large distances, they use a long, high-pitched whistle entirely unlike the sharp, short squeaks of other mice. Biologists compare this vocalization with a wolf's howl, both for its sound and for the fact that the grasshopper mouse emits it with nose raised and mouth open.

Onychomys means "clawed mouse," in reference to the long talons this rodent uses to grasp and manipulate prey. Its body is stocky, with a short, stumpy tail, small ears, and relatively short legs.

C. Allan Morgan

28 · Deer Mouse
Peromyscus maniculatus

Marty Cordano

The most widespread of all North American rodents, deer mice occupy nearly every dryland habitat, from deserts to grasslands to mountainous regions. Due to their adaptability to different environs, deer mice vary greatly in size and shape and coloration. All, however, have a two-toned tail that is dark on top and white below, like that of a white-tailed deer. And while the fine fur on their backs ranges from pale gray to reddish brown, their bellies and feet are snowy white.

The deer mouse has gained some notoriety in recent years as a host of the hantavirus that causes hantaviral pulmonary syndrome, a human disease occurring most often in the Southwest. It also hosts fleas that carry plague. The risk of people contracting either of these deadly diseases is magnified by the mouse's tendency to explore human houses and outbuildings in search of food, nesting materials, or soft places to nest.

Deer mice reproduce rapidly. In warm regions, they may breed all year, producing as many as eight litters of three to seven young. Females born in spring may become mothers themselves by late summer or early fall. Because they are so abundant, deer mice are an important food source for many small carnivores, owls, and snakes.

SIZE	Total length about 7 inches, tail 3 inches
HABITAT	Most common in grasslands but found in all life zones of the Southwest
RANGE	Widely distributed throughout much of the United States (excluding the Southeast), central Mexico, and southern Canada
ALSO KNOWN AS	wood mouse, woodland deer mouse, prairie deer mouse

29 · Cactus Mouse
Peromyscus eremicus

C. Allan Morgan

Of the many similar-looking species of *Peromyscus* found in the Southwest, the cactus mouse is most highly adapted to life in arid habitats. Relative to other members of their genus, cactus mice can forego water for longer periods of time and can tolerate higher temperatures, spreading saliva over their bodies to cool off. To conserve water and food stores, cactus mice may enter torpor on a daily basis and estivate over the summer months.

Of medium size, the cactus mouse has large eyes and ears—the better to see and hear nocturnal predators with. To blend in with sandy desert soils, its long, silky fur is typically pale gray above and buff below; populations that inhabit lava flows may be darker.

To distinguish it from other *Peromyscus,* look for the long tail, which accounts for more than half its average length. And though difficult to notice from a distance, the soles of its hind feet are completely naked to the heel.

The cactus mouse hides its grassy, fluff-lined nest in a burrow or amid rocks or clumps of cactus. Excellent climbers, they can scale cliffs and scramble up trees and bushes in search of seeds, green vegetation, and insects.

SIZE	Total length about 7.5 inches, tail 4 inches
HABITAT	Low desert areas with sandy soil and scattered vegetation; rocky outcrops
RANGE	Southern and western Arizona; into southern Nevada, California, and New Mexico, southwestern Texas; and south into Mexico
ALSO KNOWN AS	desert deer mouse

30 · American Beaver
Castor canadensis

SIZE	Total length about 39 inches, tail 16 inches; can grow to more than 60 pounds
HABITAT	Lakes, ponds, permanent streams, and slow-moving rivers bordered by trees
RANGE	Riparian areas throughout the Southwest, including the Colorado River corridor; extending throughout much of the wetlands of the United States
ALSO KNOWN AS	Canadian beaver, North American beaver

The original aquatic engineer, this large, chestnut-colored rodent alters its environment more than any other animal besides humans. It requires two things in a construction site: permanent water, such as a lake, stream, or river; and woody vegetation. By building a dam of logs, sticks, and mud, it can turn an unfavorable area into one that meets its needs for food and shelter.

After creating a pond that is suitably large and deep, the beaver either digs a burrow in the bank or builds a dome-shaped lodge of sticks and mud. Though the base and entrance holes of this fortress are submerged, the living chamber sits several inches above the water, protecting its occupants from predators and keeping them warm in the winter. The lodge typically houses a family of four to eight, consisting of a monogamous breeding pair, yearlings, and kits.

Well adapted to life in cold water and to lumberjacking, the beaver has thick, water-proof fur and webbed hind feet. It uses its distinctive paddle-shaped tail as a rudder and a warning device, slapping it on the water's surface to alert others of danger. It cuts down trees with its large, chisel-shaped incisors, eating the inner bark and using the wood for construction.

The demand for beaver pelts was a driving force behind the early exploration of western North America. By 1900, beavers were scarce. Reintroduction and protection programs have helped their populations recover in much of their original range.

Randall D. Babb

31 · Banner-tailed Kangaroo Rat
Dipodomys spectabilis

SIZE	Total length about 13 inches, tail 8 inches
HABITAT	Desert grassland with scattered shrubs and open areas easily traveled by hopping
RANGE	Throughout all but the northeastern corner of New Mexico, into west Texas, southeastern Arizona, and northern Mexico

Named for its appearance and ability to leap ten feet in a single bound, the kangaroo rat is well designed for bipedal foraging. Its center of gravity lies over its long and powerful hind legs, leaving its hands free to stuff food into external cheek pouches. Its large eyes are set back on the sides of its head, allowing it to keep watch while harvesting seed heads. By swinging its long, rudder-like tail mid-hop, it can change course abruptly, traveling in a "ricochetal" pattern to confuse predators.

The banner-tailed kangaroo rat is dark buff above, with white underparts and light eyebrows. Its distinctive tail is long and slender, ending in a "banner" of white hair set off by a black band. It dresses its fur with oil from sebaceous glands on its back, wallowing in dry sand to remove excess grease. The strange patterns left in soft wallows puzzled scientists until they recognized them as splash marks in the rodent's "bathtub."

Although its diet consists mainly of air-dried seeds, the kangaroo rat seldom drinks, even if water is available. Instead, it relies on water created as a byproduct of digesting carbohydrates.

Antisocial and aggressive, the kangaroo rat jealously guards its complex burrow and copious seed stores, warning off intruders by drumming its hind feet. Atop its burrow lies a conspicuous mound that may be ten feet across and three feet high, with up to a dozen entrances.

C. Allan Morgan

Cecil Schwalbe

Perognathus means "pouch jawed," referring to the fur-lined cheek pouches that open via slits on either side of this rodent's mouth. Though shaped much like a true mouse, the pocket mouse is more closely related to kangaroo rats and pocket gophers, which also rely on external cheek pouches to store and transport food.

The southwestern species of *Perognathus* are difficult to distinguish, thus this book discusses them as a group. The soft fur of most species is distinctly yellowish or buffy above, shading to the usual lighter or white bellies and feet. The ears are small, and the front legs short.

Together, pocket mice, kangaroo rats, and kangaroo mice comprise the most dominant family of rodents in most North American deserts and share many adaptations to life in arid climes. They subsist mainly on seeds and can endure months without drinking water. Highly efficient kidneys retain water usually lost in urination, while elongated nasal passages capture moisture otherwise lost in exhalation. When retiring to their burrows for the day, these strictly nocturnal animals plug the entrances with earth to defend against enemies and maintain humidity within the underground chambers.

SIZE	The silky pocket mouse (*P. flavus*), the smallest rodent in the Southwest, is 4 inches long with a tail slightly less than half that length The Great Basin pocket mouse (*P. parvus*) is 7 inches long, tail 3.5 inches long
HABITAT	Desert mesas and open valleys with rocky or sandy soil. Burrows found in drier locations
RANGE	Throughout the Southwest, with some local species ranging into the Great Basin and Plains

33 · Botta's Pocket Gopher
Thomomys bottae

C. Allan Morgan

Because this rodent rarely appears aboveground, it's more likely to be recognized by its home than its physical characteristics. Mounds of soil indicate an extensive burrow system that earned this solitary rodent the name gopher, from the French *guafre*, or "honeycomb." Shallow feeding tunnels connect to a deeper residential area that includes a nursery, larders, and a toilet room. When the latter has been filled, its user seals it off and excavates a new one. Active throughout the year, it may tunnel in the snow, leaving ribbons of dirt that are visible on the ground when the snow melts.

The pocket gopher is well adapted to its subterranean niche. It has a wedge-shaped head; a stout, tapering body; muscular forelegs equipped with long digging claws; small eyes and ears; and large, earth-cutting incisors. Its hair lies smooth either backward or forward, and its heavy coat often matches the color of the surrounding soil. Perhaps the most remarkable adaptation is the bare tip of the short tail—a sensory organ that feels the way when the gopher backs out of a tunnel.

T. bottae forages for roots and tubers, and sometimes pulls entire plants into its burrow. After chopping them up, the gopher transports these morsels to storage chambers in its external, fur-lined cheek pouches, or "pockets."

SIZE	Variable, with size often proportional to depth of soil. Total length averages 10 inches, tail about 3 inches
HABITAT	Almost all life zones from below sea level to above timberline. Prefers loose soil with abundant plant life. In the desert, most common along streams or near marshy spots, called *cienegas* in Spanish
RANGE	Southwestern United States and northern Mexico
ALSO KNOWN AS	valley pocket gopher, *tuza* (Spanish)

34 · Black-tailed Prairie Dog
Cynomys ludovicianus

SIZE	Total length about 15 inches, tail about 3.5 inches
HABITAT	Compact, well-drained soil in prairie grasslands
RANGE	In patches throughout the Great Plains; southwestern distribution includes all but the northwestern portion of New Mexico, into eastern Colorado, western Texas, southeastern Arizona, and northern Mexico
ALSO KNOWN AS	blacktail prairie dog

Black-tailed prairie dogs have what may be the most complex social structure of any rodent in America. Their "towns" once covered thousands of square miles and contained millions of individuals. Though they've been exterminated throughout much of their range, prairie dogs still occur in large colonies consisting of topographically based wards that are further subdivided into small breeding coteries. Members of these family groups defend their territory against outsiders but greet one another by touching incisors.

One of the most vociferous of southwestern mammals, this heavy-set ground squirrel earned its name for its repetitive bark and black-tipped tail. Trills, whistles, and chatters add to the clamor of a prairie dog town, which can be heard for some distance.

The prairie dog's deep and extensive burrow system opens via crater-shaped mounds that shed rain, induce air flow through the burrow, and provide high points from which to survey the surroundings. Individuals are often seen sitting upright on a mound, keeping an eye out for predators as others forage on grasses and forbs. When the watch-dogs sound the alarm, the squirrels dash underground, periodically peeking out to determine if the danger has passed.

An important prey species, prairie dogs feed many animals. Black-footed ferrets, in particular, have been severely affected by the tremendous reduction in prairie dog numbers.

C. Allan Morgan

35 · Red Squirrel
Tamiasciurus hudsonicus

SIZE	Total length about 13 inches, tail about 5 inches; the smallest of the tree squirrels
HABITAT	Coniferous forests, usually above 7,000 feet
RANGE	In the mountains of New Mexico, Arizona, Colorado, and Utah; extending north through the Rocky Mountains and across much of Canada, Alaska, and the northeastern United States
ALSO KNOWN AS	chickaree, pine squirrel, barking squirrel, mountain boomer, boomer

Filling the coniferous forest with barks and chatters, this vocal tree squirrel is usually heard before it is seen. When scolding intruders, it often gives a "chr-r-r, che-e-e" call that inspired the alternative common name of "chickaree." The breeding season is a particularly noisy time, as males run through each other's territories in pursuit of females, who are receptive for only one day each season.

The red squirrel dines primarily on the seeds of spruce and Douglas fir. Sitting on a favorite feeding stump or branch, it extracts nuts from cones, discarding the scales beneath it. The resulting pile of cone debris—or "kitchen midden"—becomes quite large over the years. Come summer, the squirrel harvests new cones, cutting them from the trees before the seeds can ripen and disperse, and dropping them one by one to the forest floor. It then caches these cones in its midden, where the cool dampness keeps the cones from drying out and opening.

All squirrels belong to the family *Sciuridae*, which means "shadow tail." In addition to a bushy, shadow-casting tail, the red squirrel has a black stripe on each side that separates its reddish back from its whitish belly, as well as a prominent white ring around each eye.

Marty Cordano

36 · Rock Squirrel
Spermophilus variegatus

C. Allan Morgan

Variegatus refers to the peculiar coloration of the rock squirrel's coat, the front half of the body being gray while the rear half tends toward yellowish brown. With warm weather, the heavy winter hair and undercoat shed from the head and shoulders. Before this long molting process is complete, the hind-end hair has been weathered and sunburned, giving the pelage a definite two-toned cast. The long, bushy tail rivals those of tree squirrels in beauty.

As its common name implies, this big ground squirrel frequents rocky terrain. In rimrock, the squirrel builds its nest far back in a crevice; in slide rock, the den lies deep among the tumbled mass of talus; on mesas, the squirrel excavates a winding tunnel in the earth between buried boulders. A large rock nearby provides a place where the squirrel can survey the surrounding terrain or sunbathe on cold mornings. Any perceived danger is met with a loud, shrill whistle of warning. Though this ground squirrel is a good climber, it hides underground when threatened.

Rock squirrels are voracious. Their sharp teeth and strong claws give them entrance to any cabin, where no food is safe unless encased in tin. These bold animals will climb agave stalks to reach the seed pods, seemingly oblivious to danger from red-tailed hawks. Though largely vegetarian, they rarely pass up eggs, young birds, and other meat.

SIZE	Total length about 20 inches, tail about 9 inches
HABITAT	Broken canyon country and rocky terrain from high mountains to desert edges
RANGE	Throughout the southwestern United States and northern Mexico

37 · Round-tailed Ground Squirrel
Spermophilus tereticaudus

C. Allan Morgan

This small ground squirrel received its name for its pencil-like tail. Its cinnamon-tan coat lacks the contrasting spots and stripes sported by others of its family.

The round-tailed ground squirrel is often associated with creosote bush flats, where its tawny coat blends well with the brown clay soil. Unlike its relatives, it does not climb to a vantage point to scout for danger. Instead, it will run a short distance, then settle motionless on the ground to survey the situation. If something arouses its curiosity, the animal will stand high on its hind legs to see over any low obstacle, using its tail as the third leg of a tripod for balance.

This squirrel dines primarily on green vegetation of the desert floor. Readily climbing shrubs and small trees, it often ventures shakily to the end of a limb to reach a particularly tempting bud or tip. Its diurnal activity pattern includes a fast-disappearing custom—the afternoon siesta. By 10 a.m., with a full stomach, it retires from the heat of the surface to the coolness of the burrow. By 3 p.m., as the heat begins dissipating, the roundtail re-emerges from its home until sundown.

S. tereticaudus is still relatively abundant within its limited range, but much of its former habitat has been plowed for agriculture.

SIZE	Total length about 9 inches, tail about 3 inches
HABITAT	Sonoran and Mojave Desert valleys and low mesas with alluvial soils
RANGE	Southern and eastern Arizona, into southern Nevada and California and northern Mexico
ALSO KNOWN AS	roundtail ground squirrel

$38 \cdot$ Spotted Ground Squirrel
Spermophilus spilosoma

SIZE	Total length about 9 inches, tail about 2.75 inches
HABITAT	Desert scrub and sandy grasslands of arid and semi-arid regions
RANGE	Southeastern and northern Arizona, into the Four Corners region; most of New Mexico into northern Mexico, western Texas, eastern Colorado, and the western Midwest
ALSO KNOWN AS	gopher

One of the smallest ground squirrels in North America, *S. spilosoma* is grayish-tan, with small, indistinct white spots scattered over its back. Its ears are small; its tail pencil-like and sparsely haired. Active by day, this common, widespread species is easily observed in the wild.

The spotted ground squirrel occupies some of what seems the most barren, inhospitable terrain in the Southwest. The grasslands that encompass much of its range have scant vegetation, and the rain of summer downpours quickly seeps into the thirsty surface of the soil.

Appearing rather colorless to those accustomed to the bright spots and stripes of midwestern ground squirrels, this desert-dwelling species blends perfectly with the muted colors of its habitat. It gathers seeds of all the principal desert grasses and shrubs and eats the young, tender growth of many plants. Cactus flowers and fruits are taken when available, while the pads provide food and moisture during the dry season.

This ground squirrel hides the entrance to its burrow beneath low shrubs. It hibernates in the northern part of its range, while in the southern portions it may estivate during warm months.

39 · Harris' Antelope Squirrel
Ammospermophilus harrisii

John Cancalosi

To distinguish an antelope squirrel from other members of the squirrel family, look for the conspicuous white stripe that runs along each side from shoulder to flank. In addition, the antelope squirrel runs with its tail curled over its back, displaying a lighter-colored underside. In *A. harrisii*, the bushy tail is dark gray above and a lighter mix of black and white below.

The Harris' antelope squirrel lives up to its scientific name, which means "lover of sand and seeds." A denizen of desert foothills, this rodent usually excavates its burrow among rocks. It climbs easily through cacti to dine on their fruit and seeds, sometimes staining its face and forepaws with cactus juice.

This squirrel often makes its presence known by a long, shrill trill that resembles a bird's in clarity. The approach of any real or imagined danger is greeted by violent flicks of the expressive tail and vocal expressions of disapproval.

Unlike other ground squirrels, chipmunks, and prairie dogs, this diurnal animal is active most of the year. While inclement weather will send the antelope squirrel to the shelter of its burrow, it re-emerges on sunny days. During summer and early fall, it forages early in the morning, escaping heat and drought by retreating to its cool underground burrow for most of the day.

SIZE	Total length about 9 inches, tail about 3 inches
HABITAT	Low arid desert; stony soil on alluvial fans and along rocky washes
RANGE	Throughout the southwestern half of Arizona into the extreme southwestern corner of New Mexico and northern Mexico
ALSO KNOWN AS	Harris' spermophile, marmot squirrel, gray-tailed antelope squirrel, Yuma antelope ground squirrel

SIZE	Total length about 9.5 inches, tail 4.5 inches
HABITAT	Rocky canyons with oak, juniper, or piñon along the rims
RANGE	Southeastern through northwestern Arizona, extending into Utah and eastern Nevada; in New Mexico, west of the Rio Grande; south into Mexico
ALSO KNOWN AS	gray chipmunk, gray-backed chipmunk, Gila striped squirrel, pallid chipmunk, chichimoke, chichimuka

In contrast to its prominently striped relatives, this large chipmunk has faint stripes of smoky gray on its neck and back. The heavy winter coat obscures all but the black strip down the middle of the back. Brown-and-white facial stripes are more conspicuous. The cliff chipmunk has the longest breeding season of any western chipmunk, with four to six young born between April and October.

As its name implies, the cliff chipmunk prefers rocky areas, building its nest of dried grass stems in a deep cliff crevice or under a mass of talus. Wonderfully agile and active, it nonchalantly scampers up precipitous canyon walls and overhangs. Should it fall, the bushy tail is sent in a whirling motion to slow the speed of its descent. When alarmed, it waves its tail slowly and sinuously, in contrast to the flicking motion of ground squirrels.

During the dryness of late spring and early fall, chipmunks obtain moisture from cactus fruits and berries or succulent roots and bulbs. They also eat dry grass seeds and nuts, along with an occasional insect. Because chipmunks store very little fat, they depend on cached food to see them through the winter.

C. Allan Morgan

41 · Black-tailed Jackrabbit
Lepus californicus

C. Allan Morgan

Common throughout the West, this large gray hare was dubbed "jackass rabbit" by early settlers for its outsized ears, which are tipped with black. Its current common name refers to the black stripe that runs along the top of the tail onto the rump.

Despite the "rabbit" in their names, members of this genus are technically hares. The young are born fully formed, with eyes open, and are able to hop after their mother within minutes. Rather than build a nest for her precocial young, the female hare deposits them in a grassy hollow or shallow depression scratched into the ground. They begin foraging for themselves within two weeks.

Unlike the larger antelope jackrabbit, which shares a small part of its range, the black-tailed jack doesn't often "freeze" to foil discovery. If startled by a person, this hare usually uses a slow and erratic gait, with a few unhurried leaps alternating with faster bounds. But the rush of an animal predator is met with a series of sprinting leaps that change to graceful, soaring bounds in full flight. Though the jackrabbit's racing speed cannot be matched by any native predator in the Southwest, coyotes reportedly exploit its lack of endurance by taking turns in the chase.

To thrive in desert scrubland, the jackrabbit eats the most succulent foods available, foraging in the cool of early evening and night, and dozing in the shade of low-lying vegetation by day.

SIZE	Total length about 24 inches, tail 3.5 inches; ears up to 6 inches long
HABITAT	Open, treeless areas with sparse shrub cover, such as desert scrub, grassland, and overgrazed rangeland
RANGE	Western and central United States; south through Baja and northern mainland Mexico
ALSO KNOWN AS	jackass rabbit, California jackrabbit, Great Plains jackrabbit

42 · Antelope Jackrabbit
Lepus alleni

SIZE	Total length about 30 inches, tail 2.5 inches; ears about 7 inches
HABITAT	Desert valleys and grasslands
RANGE	South central Arizona; northwestern Mexico on the west side of the Sierra Madre
ALSO KNOWN AS	Allen's hare, Allen's jackrabbit, Mexican jackrabbit

Large and fast, this hare was named for the bounding flash of white derriere resembling that of a pronghorn in flight. When the jackrabbit is undisturbed, its gray guard hairs cover the white rump patch, and the animal blends into a background of dry grass and adobe soil. But when the hare runs, specialized white, erectile hairs on the hip facing its pursuer stand up. The hips seem to flicker on and off as the animal abruptly turns, always keeping the conspicuous white patch in view.

Another distinguishing feature of the antelope jackrabbit is the huge, white-fringed ears, which account for a quarter of the animal's surface area. In addition to providing keen hearing, these ears may help the hare dissipate heat.

The antelope jackrabbit lives in the most arid parts of Arizona, among valleys and hills covered with drought-resistant shrubs and trees. It eats grasses and herbs, adding moisture to its diet with cactus pads.

Although it can run at more than forty miles per hour, this rabbit usually freezes to evade detection rather than leave its resting place. When choosing to flee, it soars gracefully through the air in a series of arcs, sinking to the ground only to leave again in undulating bounds covering ten to fifteen feet. At high speed, the hind feet hit the ground about two yards in front of the forefeet, producing a rocking motion and a distinctive track.

43 · Desert Cottontail
Sylvilagus audubonii

Named for the pure white undersides of their fluffy tails, which they flash when fleeing, cottontails are similar across the United States. This desert species is widespread and abundant throughout lower elevations of the Southwest. Its buff gray back blends well with its arid surroundings, and its ears are relatively large.

Cottontail rabbits belong to the same taxonomic order as hares and pikas. They are not rodents, as was once assumed. In fact, these vegetarians are probably more closely related to deer and elk.

Like other rabbits—and unlike hares—the desert cottontail rears its young in a carefully constructed nest. The female lines a shallow, pear-shaped burrow with grass and fur that she plucks from her belly. Newborn rabbits are blind and hairless, comparatively helpless until their eyes open. Their progress is then so rapid that they are able to leave the nest at about three weeks and begin breeding by the age of three months. An adult female may bear several litters of several young each year.

Cottontail populations are kept in check by nearly every carnivore of half their size or more, from rattlesnakes to raptors to other mammals. Though fast on their feet, they do not rely entirely on speed to avoid capture. Instead, they make a zigzag dash for the nearest burrow or clump of brush in which to hide.

SIZE	Total length about 15 inches, tail about 2 inches; ears 2 to 3 inches
HABITAT	Adapted to a variety of habitats; generally found wherever sufficient cover is available
RANGE	Throughout the Southwest at elevations up to 5,000 feet; also occurs across the western portion of the Plains states
ALSO KNOWN AS	Audubon's cottontail, prairie-dog rabbit

44 · Nine-banded Armadillo
Dasypus novemcinctus

SIZE	Total length about 30 inches, tail about 14 inches
HABITAT	Brushy areas with soft loamy or sandy soils
RANGE	In the Southwest, limited to portions of western Texas and possibly southeastern New Mexico; well distributed from northern South America throughout much of Mexico, penetrating Texas east to Florida and as far north as Nebraska
ALSO KNOWN AS	long-nosed armadillo

In Spanish, *armadillo* means "little armored one" in reference to the bony shell that encases its upper parts and tail. No other mammal possesses a similar protective coating, which actually consists of modified skin. Between the large shields that cover this species' shoulder and rump are nine bands of bony plates mounted on a flexible base that allows the body to curl into a ball.

Related most closely to sloths and anteaters, armadillos occur primarily in the tropics. This species alone extends into the southern United States, where it has been expanding its range northward and eastward over the past century. It apparently cannot tolerate long periods of either drought or freezing weather. In arid areas, the armadillo frequents waterholes and streams to drink and take mud baths. It also adjusts its activity pattern seasonally to take advantage of cool nights in the summer and warm afternoons in the winter, retreating to an underground burrow to escape temperature extremes.

The armadillo dines mainly on insects and other invertebrates, relying on its keen sense of smell to locate food. It employs its pointed nose for rooting, long claws for digging, and sticky tongue for snaring prey. The armadillo's reputation for raiding gardens and bird's nests is largely unfounded.

This species usually gives birth to identical quadruplets that develop from a single fertilized egg. Newborns are covered with a soft, leathery skin that gradually hardens into the characteristic bony carapace.

Erwin and Peggy Bauer

45 · Southern Long-nosed Bat
Leptonycteris curasoae

Because of their secretive habits and nocturnal lifestyles, bats have long been victims of fear and superstition. Fortunately, our understanding of these unaggressive creatures has grown rapidly in recent decades. Among other things, ecologists have discovered that bats play an important role in controlling insect populations, pollinating plants, and dispersing seeds.

The only mammals capable of true flight, bats belong to the order Chiroptera, which means "hand wing." Thin membranes of skin stretch between greatly elongated fingers, and to arms, body, and legs, forming maneuverable wings. Many species also have a membrane connecting the legs and tail.

Equipped with remarkably acute hearing, many bats navigate to avoid obstacles and locate prey in total darkness by listening to echoes of their own cries. These are often above the range of human hearing. Experiments have shown that bats with blocked ears or mouths lose the ability to echolocate and become disoriented rapidly. Fruit- and nectar-eating bats, such as *L. curasoae*, also employ smell and vision to find their food.

Merlin D. Tuttle

Many plants of the Sonoran Desert depend heavily on the southern long-nosed bat for pollination. Like a nocturnal hummingbird, it can hover near a blossom, inserting its slender snout and lapping up nectar and pollen with the fleshy bristles on its tongue. A summertime resident of the Southwest, it migrates from Mexico, apparently following the flowering cycles of agave, along with saguaro, organ pipe, and other cacti. It also eats the pulp of cactus fruits.

This grayish-brown bat roosts in caves and mine shafts, where females form large maternal colonies during the summer birthing season.

SIZE	Total length about 3 inches, external tail absent
HABITAT	In the Southwest, occurs mainly in desert scrub and grassland
RANGE	Southern Arizona and southwestern most New Mexico; into Mexico
ALSO KNOWN AS	Sanborn's long-nosed bat, little long-nosed bat, lesser long-nosed bat

46 · Brazilian Free-tailed Bat
Tadarida brasiliensis

SIZE	Total length about 4 inches, tail about 1.3 inches
HABITAT	Caves, cliff crevices, hollow trees, mine tunnels, buildings, and bridges from high mountains to low desert
RANGE	Throughout the southern half of the United States and most of Mexico
ALSO KNOWN AS	Mexican free-tailed bat, Mexican freetail bat, house bat, guano bat

Perhaps the most common bat in the Southwest, *T. brasiliensis* congregates in caves and caverns. It may form colonies of many millions, the largest known for any mammal. The famous sunset flights at Carlsbad Caverns National Park consist primarily of Brazilian free-tailed bats pouring out to spend the night hunting for moths and other insects. A single bat may consume more than half its body mass in insects each night; a summer colony plays an important role in controlling insects over a large area.

Although some free-tailed bats remain in this region during winter months, most migrate to central and southern Mexico. They breed there, then return to rear their young. Females give birth to a single baby in mid-June, with most of the young arriving within a two-week span. The young are deposited together in a large nursery away from the males. The mothers return from their nocturnal foraging flights to nurse, picking out their own pup from among thousands by a combination of smell, sound, and location. In the incubator-like environment of the nursery, the young grow rapidly and can fly out to feed on their own within six weeks.

Free-tailed bats are named for the portion of the tail that extends well beyond the short tail membrane. *T. brasiliensis* is a medium-sized, dark-colored bat, with wide, flattened ears that extend forward over the eyes. Its long, narrow wings make it among the fastest of all bats; its rapid, powerful flight is similar to that of swifts.

Merlin D. Tuttle

47 · Pallid Bat
Antrozous pallidus

Merlin D. Tuttle

As its common name implies, this is a light-colored bat, blonde above and white below. Its sandy coat helps it blend with the desert floor, where its prominent ears aid in detecting prey.

Unlike most others in its family, which capture small flying insects on the wing, the pallid bat specializes in larger, ground-dwelling prey. It flies low, often landing on the ground to grab a beetle or grasshopper. The pallid bat is even known to eat scorpions and centipedes, along with an occasional lizard or pocket mouse. A pollinator of various cacti, this bat likely visits such flowers to feed on the insects found within.

To add to its unusual dining habits, the pallid bat carries its larger prey to a feeding roost, such as a shallow cave or house porch, where it eats the soft parts and drops the hard wings and legs. By day, it roosts with others in crevices among rocks or in buildings.

This species mates in the fall while the bats are gathering to hibernate. The female stores the sperm in her reproductive tract until spring, when she ovulates, and the eggs are fertilized. In May and June, females form large maternal colonies, where they give birth to and raise their litter of one or two.

SIZE	Total length about 4.5 inches, tail about 1.8 inches
HABITAT	From low deserts to high mountains; most common in dry areas with rocky outcrops
RANGE	Throughout the western United States and northern Mexico
ALSO KNOWN AS	desert bat

48· Western Pipistrelle
Pipistrellus hesperus

SIZE	Total length 2.8 inches, tail 1.3 inches
HABITAT	Desert scrub and grassland; prefers rocky cliffs along watercourses
RANGE	Throughout the southwestern United States and northern Mexico
ALSO KNOWN AS	canyon bat

North America's smallest bat, the western pipistrelle weighs about as much as a nickel. Its black nose, ears, and legs contrast sharply with its ashy gray fur, and its long tail is almost completely enclosed within the tail membrane.

This bat has a slow, fluttering flight somewhat like that of a butterfly. Commonly seen near desert watercourses and watering holes, it begins foraging early in the evening, often before sunset. It usually feeds within swarms of small insects, gorging on whatever is seasonally available.

Though very agile, the western pipistrelle is not a strong flyer and cannot venture far from permanent water. It roosts alone or with a few others in cliffside crevices or rocky outcrops, typically along canyon drainages. The window shutters and patio ceilings of homes with swimming pools provide additional roosting sites. It hibernates in cold weather, presumably not far from where it spends the summer.

Whereas most bats give birth to a single pup each year, the western pipistrelle typically has two. The female delivers her young in a head-up position, catching the babies in her tail membrane.

Merlin D. Tuttle

49 · Desert Shrew
Notiosorex crawfordi

SIZE	Total length less than 4 inches, tail slightly more than 1 inch
HABITAT	Primarily semi-arid desert shrub; apparently not restricted to any particular habitat
RANGE	Throughout most of the Southwest except a portion of southwestern Arizona
ALSO KNOWN AS	gray shrew

Due to its small size and secretive habits, the desert shrew presents a challenge to biologists, who know relatively little about its life history and behavior in the wild. Like other shrews, it has a long, pointed nose and small, rudimentary eyes. Its fur is a dark bluish-gray on top, lighter underneath, and its ears are prominent for a shrew.

The shrew's story is that of an appetite mounted on four legs, guided by a keen nose and aided by formidable claws and teeth. A tiny animal, it loses a great deal of heat through its relatively large body surface area. To compensate, this ferocious insectivore must spend a great portion of its short life hunting and eating, as it would starve to death if it went more than half a day without food. Between bouts of seemingly frantic activity, the shrew enters a deep, torpor-like sleep.

Found in a wide range of habitats, this shrew seems to prefer sites that provide a somewhat humid microclimate in the desert, such as boulder fields, brushpiles, beehives, and woodrat nests. It forages under vegetation; signs might be found in leaf mold under desert trees and shrubs, and in grasslands where tiny tunnels weave through tangled stems. Though the desert shrew can obtain all the moisture it needs from the soft body parts of its prey and other food, it will drink if water is available.

Cecil Schwalbe

Marty Cordano

The only marsupial native to the United States, the opossum would be difficult to mistake for any other animal. About the size of a house cat, it has a long, pointed snout with a rather bulbous pink nose and a prehensile tail that is long and hairless. Its shaggy fur is generally gray to black, lighter about the face, and black on the feet. The big toes on its hind feet are opposable.

Didelphis means "two wombs." One of these likely refers to the female's abdominal pouch, which encloses a single mammary gland with thirteen nipples. After a gestation of less than two weeks, up to twenty-one bean-sized babies are born, blind, naked, and poorly developed. The young pull themselves to the fur-lined pouch, where those that can't attach themselves to nipples will die. Once a baby begins to nurse, the nipple swells to fill its mouth, keeping it firmly affixed to its mother for the first two months. After the young detach and emerge, the pouch serves as traveling nursery for some time.

The opossum's jaws are studded with 50 sharp teeth, more than any other native mammal. Although formidable weapons, the teeth are rarely used when the opossum is faced with danger. If unable to run for cover, it will "play possum," or feign death. Its heartbeat slows, its muscles become limp, and it may emit a putrid-smelling discharge from its anal glands. Although the opossum appears lifeless, it will come out of this catatonic state if left alone.

SIZE	Total length about 30 inches, tail about 12 inches
HABITAT	In the Southwest, limited mostly to deciduous woodland along streams and rivers
RANGE	Abundant throughout the eastern and central regions of the United States and Mexico, the opossum's occurrence in the southwestern states is limited to portions of western Texas, eastern Colorado, central-eastern New Mexico, and southern Arizona; its range is expanding westward
ALSO KNOWN AS	opossum, possum

SUGGESTED READING

Burt, William H., and Richard P. Grossenheider. 1998. *A Field Guide to the Mammals: North America North of Mexico*. Boston: Peterson Field Guides, Houghton Mifflin.

Cockrum, E. Lendell, and Yar Petryszyn. 1992. *Mammals of the Southwestern United States and Northwestern Mexico*. Tucson: Treasure Chest Publications.

Davis, William B., and David J. Schmidly. 1994. *The Mammals of Texas*. Austin: Texas Parks and Wildlife Press. Online edition: www.nsrl.ttu.edu/tmot1

Jones, Clyde, Robert S. Hoffmann, Dale W. Rice, Robert J. Baker, Mark D. Engstrom, Robert D. Bradley, David J. Schmidly, and Cheri A. Jones. 1997. *Revised Checklist of North American Mammals North of Mexico, 1997*. Occasional Paper Number 173. Lubbock: Museum of Texas Tech University.

Larson, Peggy. 2000. *A Sierra Club Naturalist's Guide to the Deserts of the Southwest*. San Francisco: Sierra Club Press.

National Geographic Society. 1995. *Wild Animals of North America*. Washington, D.C.: National Geographic Society.

Stall, Chris. 1989. *Animal Tracks of the Rocky Mountains*. Seattle: The Mountaineers.

Whitaker, J. O., Jr. 1996. *The Audubon Society Field Guide to North American Mammals*. New York: Alfred A. Knopf.

Wilson, Don E., and Sue Ruff, eds. *The Smithsonian Book of North American Mammals*. 1999. Washington and London: Smithsonian Institution Press.

Zeveloff, Samuel I. 1988. *Mammals of the Intermountain West*. Salt Lake City: University of Utah Press.

INDEX